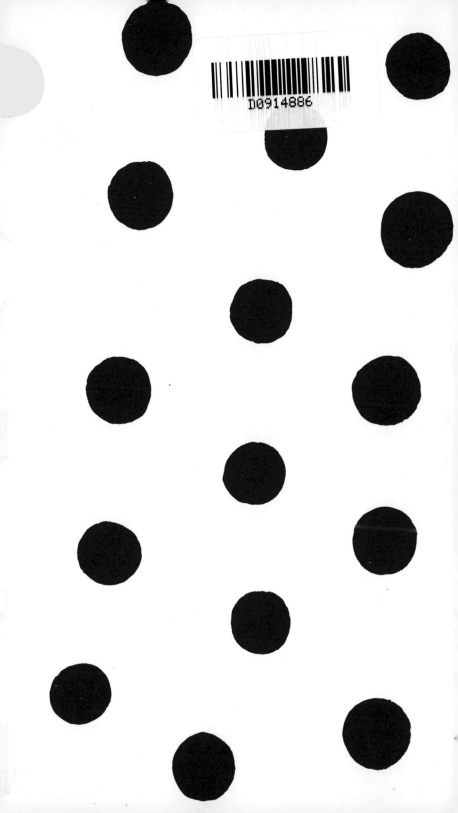

D0914886

Old Chestnuts
Warmed Up

Deaf Betty — warming the wrong Bed.

Deaf Betty warming the wrong bed
George Cruikshank from the Murray visitors' book, 1830

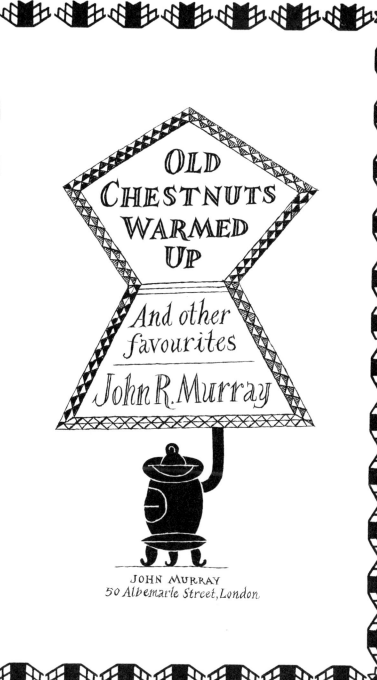

OLD
CHESTNUTS
WARMED
UP

And other
favourites

John R. Murray

JOHN MURRAY
50 Albemarle Street, London

Virginia
for her inspiration

Wood engraving above: Reynolds Stone
Title page and endpapers: Jeff Fisher
Title page border: Curwen Press

This volume has been compiled,
designed and edited by John R. Murray
and typeset by Tom Milligan

© This selection: John R. Murray 1997

First published in 1997
by John Murray (Publishers) Ltd
50 Albemarle Street, London W1X 4BD

Reprinted 1997

All rights reserved
Unauthorized duplication
contravenes applicable laws

The moral right of the author has been asserted

A catalogue record of this book is available
from the British Library
ISBN 0-7195-5839-5

Typeset in Monotype Walbaum 12pt
Printed and bound in Great Britain by
The University Press, Cambridge

CONTENTS

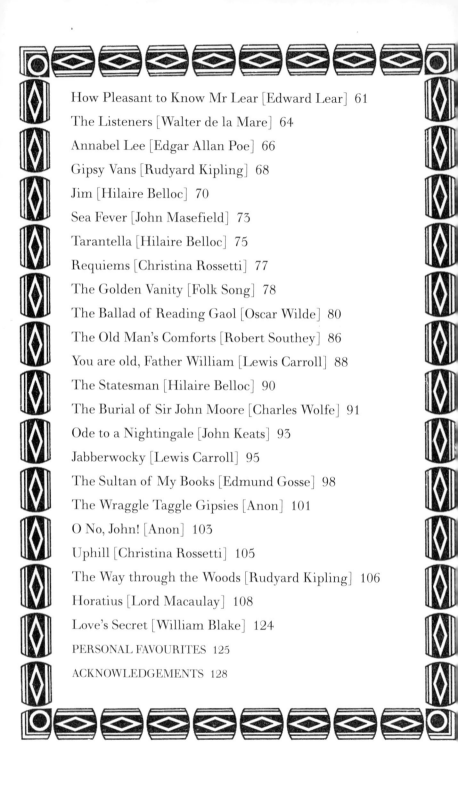

Charles Darwin delivering his contribution
to 50 Albemarle Street, *c.*1859
Val Biro

INTRODUCTION

This volume gathers together a very personal collection of mostly old-fashioned verse which I have memorized either in whole or in part and which has given me enormous pleasure. The idea is to encourage those who dip into it to make their own selection and to share it with family and friends. It is purely for enjoyment.

Why Memorize Verse?

The English master at my prep school was besotted by Macaulay. We were set great chunks of 'Horatius' to learn by heart and on one occasion I, with two friends, was chosen to recite the Holding of the Bridge. The scene was as follows: Mr Elliott, our master, stood facing down the gangway between the two blocks of classroom desks. I was called out and commenced: 'Lars Porsena of Clusium by the Nine Gods he swore . . .' Mr Elliott then took up the position of Horatius standing four square before us. My friend took over:

> Meanwhile the Tuscan army,
>   Right glorious to behold,
> Came flashing back the noonday light,
> Rank behind rank, like surges bright
>   Of a broad sea of gold.

After some fierce skirmishing, I stepped forward as 'the great Lord of Luna', in my schoolboy shorts, and raised my imaginary broadsword:

> Then, whirling up his broadsword
>   With both hands to the height,
> He rushed against Horatius,
>   And smote with all his might.

Mr Elliott deflected the imaginary blow to his head but staggered as if struck on the thigh. Then, regaining his strength, he raised his sword above his head and cut me down. I fell to the ground and the refrain was taken up by the next boy. At this point the bridge behind Horatius was heard to collapse and Mr Elliott dived under his desk as if plunging into the Tiber. Thus ended 'Horatius' for the day.

This was my first experience of memorizing narrative verse and whenever I hear 'Horatius' (which is not often as Macaulay is so out of fashion) I think of Mr Elliott playing out his heroic role.

From then on throughout my time at school we were made to learn poetry and recite it in class. It was never such fun again and our main reason for making an effort was usually to avoid trouble rather than to understand or enjoy the poems themselves.

After leaving school and before going up to Oxford I went to Grenoble to learn French. I stayed with a family of 15 children (a product of de Gaulle's policy of offering everything free to all children after the fourth, to help

populate France). Not fitting easily into the Summer
University regime, I hired a bicycle and rode out into
the hills where, finding a remote spot, I would lie in the
grass learning or remembering verse. Much came back
to me easily because of the efforts I had made at school.
I remember particularly the pleasure of reciting 'Leisure'
by William Henry Davies: 'What is this life if, full of care,
We have no time to stand and stare'. As I had just escaped
from the whirl of the city and was now in an apple orchard
on a hillside, this suited my mood perfectly.

Not long after this I moved on to stay in the Pyrenees
and joined a friend high up in the hills in the little village
of Eusa. There, when dipping into an anthology of verse,
I came across an old favourite, 'Tarantella':

> Do you remember an Inn,
> Miranda?
> Do you remember an Inn?
> And the tedding and the spreading
> Of the straw for a bedding,
> And the fleas that tease in the High Pyrenees . . .

When I now recite it, I always think back to that strange
medieval village where the priest used to take confession
in the tiny square wearing an enormous black cloak and
summoning each family in turn to him.

I soon came to realize how easy it was to find verse to
reflect and enhance one's mood and it was at this time that
my godmother Freya Stark, that well-known traveller, gave

me a copy of Wavell's *Other Men's Flowers*, the anthology of all the verse he could recite by heart and which sustained him so well while in command in the desert during the war. He writes in his Foreword that he learnt old favourites rather than 'fresh poets', and it is this that makes his anthology so special — although perhaps to some rather old-fashioned. As he says, 'One of my charges against modern poetry is that it does not easily lend itself to memorizing or declamation.'

I went to stay with Freya in a beautiful wooden house on the edge of the Bosphorus, upstream from Istanbul on the Asiatic shore — a place called Kandhyli (made memorable by Harold Nicolson in *Sweet Waters*). There I tried to learn a little Turkish from Mustapha, her teacher, so that I could make my way across Anatolia safely. After travelling for some weeks I arrived on the Carian shore. In the early evening, as I sat on a headland looking out to sea, I watched the sun slowly dropping below the horizon and as it did I recited 'Heraclitus' which includes these two lines:

> I wept as I remembered how often you and I
> Had tired the sun with talking and sent him
> > > down the sky.

Somehow as I spoke these words I felt more a part of the landscape and its history and less of an intruder. This is something that the reciting of verse can do in its right place, and which all the poems in this slim volume have offered me at one time or another.

11

Some poems, although only learnt later in life, carry me back vividly to earlier days. One example is Robert Louis Stevenson's 'The Lamplighter'. When I was small I used to go to tea with my godfather who lived in Great Ormond Street. In winter as it got dark I would look out of the window and see the old lamplighter on his bicycle zigzagging up the street with his long pole, turning on the gas lights as he passed each lampstand. I now always imagine him as Old Leerie:

> For every night at teatime and before you take
> your seat,
> With lantern and with ladder he comes posting up
> the street ...
> For we are very lucky, with a lamp before the door,
> And Leerie stops to light it as he lights so many more.

I was lucky that my mother used to sing to us before we went to sleep. Two songs which I particularly remember are 'O No, John!' and 'The Wraggle Taggle Gipsies'. These I never needed to learn as my mother imprinted them on our minds. However, as children we were intrigued by gypsy lore because Walter Starkie, that remarkable Irish scholar and follower of gypsies, used to come to stay. Of a summer evening when we were in bed he would step out on to the terrace beneath our window and play the most haunting gypsy melodies on his fiddle. Sometimes a string would snap. He would then tie a knot in it, retune it and continue to play. He told us many stories of the gypsies in Spain and Transylvania and I particularly remember him reciting:

Unless you come of the gipsy stock
  That steal by night and day,
Lock your heart with a double lock
  And throw the key away.

Living in Hampstead we would often walk down the Heath to Keats' House where we would be shown the tree on which the famous nightingale was said to have perched. Whether it did or not, 'Ode to a Nightingale' always reminds me of it, and I can see every twig in my mind's eye and imagine Keats listening close by.

Another poem that carries me back to Hampstead (although I suppose it should be to Stoke Poges) is 'Gray's Elegy' – my ancestor was one of those who combined to give the original manuscript to Eton College. I used to walk down from our house beside the Heath to the Vale of Health to visit the 'matchbox of a house' in which Leigh Hunt and his family lived. From there I would follow his footsteps up over the Heath towards Highgate, a path he took when going to meet Coleridge. On a summer evening I would sit at the highest point from where I could see the spire of Highgate church on the top of its hill ahead, and behind, if lucky, the spire of Christ Church, Hampstead, just visible through the trees. Sitting there I would learn 'Gray's Elegy' by heart which seemed to suit the mood exactly:

The curfew tolls the knell of parting day,
The lowing herd wind slowly o'er the lea,
The ploughman homeward plods his weary way,
And leaves the world to darkness and to me.

And on occasion the 'moping owl' kindly played its part.

While at Oxford I came across the Hesketh Pearson biography of Oscar Wilde which is full of Wilde's *bon mots*, so useful to undergraduates wanting to impress at dinner. However Hesketh Pearson also introduced me to 'The Ballad of Reading Gaol' and this probably had more influence on me than any other poem at the time. I was haunted by the poor man who was to swing, and whenever I passed Oxford Gaol I thought of him:

> I never saw a man who looked
>   With such a wistful eye
> Upon that little tent of blue
>   Which prisoners call the sky.

It is easy to continue reminiscing through poetry, verse and occasional doggerel though it may become tedious for others. However, I will just add one more memory. I decided when I first fell in love with a girl I met at Oxford that the way to win her over was to recite Andrew Marvell's 'To His Coy Mistress' to her, choosing the moment carefully. She invited me to stay at her parents' house one weekend and when I thought all was well I wandered with her to the summerhouse. There I declaimed this marvellous poem to perfection (or so it seemed to me). I approached the key moment with great hopes of success but these were shattered when she made it clear to me that she had no fear of 'Time's wingèd chariot' and felt that it should play no part in the equation. Although I lost her I still bless her for inspiring me to learn the poem by heart.

OLD CHESTNUTS
and Other Favourites

Cormorant with bag and bears
Peter Campbell

Birds, Bags, Bears and Buns

[ANON]

The common cormorant or shag
Lays eggs inside a paper bag.
The reason you will see, no doubt,
It is to keep the lightning out,
But what these unobservant birds
Have never noticed is that herds
Of wandering bears may come with buns
And steal the bags to hold the crumbs.

The Lamplighter

[ROBERT LOUIS STEVENSON]

My tea is nearly ready and the sun has left the sky;
It's time to take the window to see Leerie going by;
For every night at teatime and before you take your seat,
With lantern and with ladder he comes posting up the
                                       street.

Now Tom would be a driver and Maria go to sea,
And my papa's a banker and as rich as he can be;
But I, when I am stronger and can choose what I'm to do,
O Leerie, I'll go round at night and light the lamps with
                                       you!

For we are very lucky, with a lamp before the door,
And Leerie stops to light it as he lights so many more;
And O! before you hurry by with ladder and with light,
O Leerie, see a little child and nod to him tonight!

The Nightmare

[W.S. GILBERT]

When you're lying awake with a dismal headache, and
     repose is taboo'd by anxiety,
I conceive you may use any language you choose to
     indulge in, without impropriety;
For your brain is on fire – the bedclothes conspire of usual
     slumber to plunder you:
First your counterpane goes, and uncovers your toes, and
     your sheet slips demurely from under you;
Then the blanketing tickles – you feel like mixed pickles –
     so terribly sharp is the pricking,
And you're hot, and you're cross, and you tumble and toss
     till there's nothing 'twixt you and the tickling.
Then the bedclothes all creep to the ground in a heap, and
     you pick 'em all up in a tangle;
Next your pillow resigns and politely declines to remain at
     its usual angle!
Well, you get some repose in the form of a doze, with hot
     eye-balls and head ever aching,
But your slumbering teems with such horrible dreams that
     you'd very much better be waking;
For you dream you are crossing the Channel, and tossing
     about in a steamer from Harwich –
Which is something between a large bathing machine and
     a very small second-class carriage –

And you're giving a treat (penny ice and cold meat) to a
    party of friends and relations –
They're a ravenous horde – and they all came on board at
    Sloane Square and Kensington Stations.
And bound on that journey you find your attorney (who
    started that morning from Devon);
He's a bit undersized, and you don't feel surprised when he
    tells you he's only eleven.
Well, you're driving like mad with this singular lad
    (by-the-bye the ship's now a four-wheeler),
And you're playing round games, and he calls you bad
    names when you tell him that 'ties pay the dealer';
But this you can't stand, so you throw up your hand, and
    you find you're as cold as an icicle,
In your shirt and your socks (the black silk with gold
    clocks), crossing Salisbury Plain on a bicycle:
And he and the crew are on bicycles too – which they've
    somehow or other invested in –
And he's telling the tars, all the particu*lars* of a company
    he's interested in –
It's a scheme of devices, to get at low prices, all goods from
    cough mixtures to cables
(Which tickled the sailors) by treating retailers, as though
    they were all vege*ta*bles –
You get a good spadesman to plant a small tradesman,
    (first take off his boots with a boot-tree),
And his legs will take root, and his fingers will shoot, and
    they'll blossom and bud like a fruit-tree –
From the greengrocer tree you get grapes and green pea,
    cauliflower, pineapple, and cranberries,

While the pastrycook plant, cherry brandy will grant,
    apple puffs, and three-corners, and banberries –
The shares are a penny, and ever so many are taken by
    Rothschild and Baring,
And just as a few are allotted to you, you awake with a
    shudder despairing –
You're a regular wreck, with a crick in your neck, and no
    wonder you snore, for your head's on the floor, and
    you've needles and pins from your soles to your shins,
    and your flesh is a-creep for your left leg's asleep, and
    you've cramp in your toes, and a fly on your nose,
    and some fluff in your lung, and a feverish tongue,
    and a thirst that's intense, and a general sense that you
    haven't been sleeping in clover;
But the darkness has passed, and it's daylight at last, and
    the night has been long – ditto ditto my song – and
    thank goodness they're both of them over!

His Book's Patron

[MARTIAL]

To whom shalt Thou be dedicate?
Get thee a patron e'er it's late –
My Book – ere thou, without a friend,
Into the kitchen's deeps descend,
To wrap up spices for the pot,
Or shroud a fish *en papillotte*!

Faustinus! Him for friend you've found?
Wise book that shalt go bravely bound,
Fragrant, with painted bosses graced,
In dainty purple all embraced,
And with red title-page! My Book,
Fear neither Critics nor the Cook!

After Blenheim

[ROBERT SOUTHEY]

It was a summer evening,
   Old Kaspar's work was done,
And he before his cottage door
   Was sitting in the sun,
And by him sported on the green
His little grandchild Wilhelmine.

She saw her brother Peterkin
   Roll something large and round
Which he beside the rivulet
   In playing there had found;
He came to ask what he had found
That was so large and smooth and round.

Old Kaspar took it from the boy
   Who stood expectant by;
And then the old man shook his head,
   And with a natural sigh
'"Tis some poor fellow's skull,' said he,
'Who fell in the great victory.

'I find them in the garden,
  For there's many here about;
And often when I go to plough
  The ploughshare turns them out.
For many thousand men,' said he,
'Were slain in that great victory.'

'Now tell us what 'twas all about,'
  Young Peterkin he cries;
And little Wilhelmine looks up
  With wonder-waiting eyes;
'Now tell us all about the war,
And what they fought each other for.'

'It was the English,' Kaspar cried,
  'Who put the French to rout;
But what they fought each other for
  I could not well make out.
But every body said,' quoth he,
'That 'twas a famous victory.

'My father lived at Blenheim then,
  Yon little stream hard by;
They burnt his dwelling to the ground,
  And he was forced to fly:
So with his wife and child he fled,
Nor had he where to rest his head.

'With fire and sword the country round
  Was wasted far and wide,
And many a childing mother then
  And newborn baby died:
But things like that, you know, must be
At every famous victory.

'They say it was a shocking sight
  After the field was won;
For many thousand bodies here
  Lay rotting in the sun:
But things like that, you know, must be
After a famous victory.

'Great praise the Duke of Marlbro' won
  And our good Prince Eugene;'
'Why 'twas a very wicked thing!'
  Said little Wilhelmine;
'Nay . . nay . . my little girl,' quoth he,
'It was a famous victory.

'And every body praised the Duke
  Who this great fight did win.'
'But what good came of it at last?'
  Quoth little Peterkin.
'Why that I cannot tell,' said he,
'But 'twas a famous victory.'

The Frog

[HILAIRE BELLOC]

Be kind and tender to the Frog,
  And do not call him names,
As 'Slimy skin', or 'Polly-wog',
  Or likewise 'Ugly James',
Or 'Gape-a-grin', or 'Toad-gone-wrong',
  Or 'Billy Bandy-knees':
The Frog is justly sensitive
  To epithets like these.
No animal will more repay
  A treatment kind and fair;
At least so lonely people say
Who keep a frog (and, by the way,
  They are extremely rare).

The Frog chatting with a millipede
Unknown artist

When I was One-and-Twenty

[A.E. HOUSMAN]

When I was one-and-twenty
    I heard a wise man say,
'Give crowns and pounds and guineas
    But not your heart away;
Give pearls away and rubies
    But keep your fancy free.'
But I was one-and-twenty,
    No use to talk to me.

When I was one-and-twenty
    I heard him say again,
'The heart out of the bosom
    Was never given in vain;
'Tis paid with sighs a plenty
    And sold for endless rue.'
And I am two-and-twenty,
    And oh, 'tis true, 'tis true.

Lochinvar

[WALTER SCOTT]

O, young Lochinvar is come out of the west,
Through all the wide Border his steed was the best;
And save his good broadsword he weapons had none,
He rode all unarm'd, and he rode all alone.
So faithful in love, and so dauntless in war,
There never was knight like the young Lochinvar.

He staid not for brake, and he stopp'd not for stone,
He swam the Eske river where ford there was none;
But ere he alighted at Netherby gate,
The bride had consented, the gallant came late:
For a laggard in love, and a dastard in war,
Was to wed the fair Ellen of brave Lochinvar.

So boldly he enter'd the Netherby Hall,
Among bride's-men, and kinsmen, and brothers, and all:
Then spoke the bride's father, his hand on his sword,
(For the poor craven bridegroom said never a word,)
'O come ye in peace here, or come ye in war,
Or to dance at our bridal, young Lord Lochinvar?' –

'I long woo'd your daughter, my suit you denied; —
Love swells like the Solway, but ebbs like its tide —
And now am I come, with this lost love of mine,
To lead but one measure, drink one cup of wine.
There are maidens in Scotland more lovely by far,
That would gladly be bride to the young Lochinvar.'

The bride kiss'd the goblet: the knight took it up,
He quaff'd off the wine, and he threw down the cup.
She look'd down to blush, and she look'd up to sigh,
With a smile on her lips, and a tear in her eye.
He took her soft hand, ere her mother could bar, —
'Now tread we a measure!' said young Lochinvar.

So stately his form, and so lovely her face,
That never a hall such a galliard did grace;
While her mother did fret, and her father did fume,
And the bridegroom stood dangling his bonnet and plume,
And the bride-maidens whisper'd, ''Twere better by far,
To have match'd our fair cousin with young Lochinvar.'

One touch to her hand, and word in her ear,
When they reach'd the hall-door, and the charger stood near;
So light to the croupe the fair lady he swung,
So light to the saddle before her he sprung!
'She is won! We are gone, over bank, bush, and scaur;
They'll have fleet steeds that follow,' quoth young Lochinvar.

There was mounting 'mong Græmes of the Netherby clan;
Forsters, Fenwicks, and Musgraves, they rode and they ran;
There was racing and chasing, on Cannobie Lee,
But the lost bride of the Netherby ne'er did they see.
So daring in love, and so dauntless in war,
Have ye e'er heard of gallant like young Lochinvar.

Parr's Life Pills

[ANON]

'Twas in the town of Lubeck,
  A hundred years ago,
An old man walk'd into the church,
  With beard as white as snow;
Yet were his cheeks not wrinkled,
  Nor dim his eagle eye:
There's many a knight that steps the street,
Might wonder, should he chance to meet
  That man erect and high!

When silenced was the organ,
  And hush'd the vespers loud,
The Sacristan approach'd the sire,
  And drew him from the crowd –
There's something in thy visage,
  On which I dare not look,
And when I rang the passing bell,
A tremor that I may not tell,
  My very vitals shook.

Who art thou, awful stranger?
  Our ancient annals say,
That twice two hundred years ago
  Another pass'd this way,

32

Like thee in face and feature;
  And, if the tale be true,
'Tis writ, that in this very year
Again the stranger shall appear.
  Art thou the Wandering Jew?'

'The Wandering Jew, thou dotard!'
  The wondrous phantom cried –
''Tis several centuries ago
  Since that poor stripling died.
He would not use my nostrums –
  See, shaveling here they are!
These put to flight all human ills,
These conquer death – unfailing pills,
  And I'm the inventor, PARR!'

Parr with the Sacristan
Richard Doyle

Evening on Hampstead Heath
from *Old and New London*

From Elegy
Written in a Country Churchyard
[THOMAS GRAY]

The curfew tolls the knell of parting day,
The lowing herd wind slowly o'er the lea,
The ploughman homeward plods his weary way,
And leaves the world to darkness and to me.

Now fades the glimmering landscape on the sight,
And all the air a solemn stillness holds,
Save where the beetle wheels his droning flight,
And drowsy tinklings lull the distant folds;

Save that from yonder ivy-mantled tower
The moping owl does to the moon complain
Of such as, wandering near her secret bower,
Molest her ancient solitary reign.

Beneath those rugged elms, that yew-tree's shade,
Where heaves the turf in many a mouldering heap,
Each in his narrow cell for ever laid,
The rude forefathers of the hamlet sleep.

The breezy call of incense-breathing morn,
The swallow twittering from the straw-built shed,
The cock's shrill clarion or the echoing horn,
No more shall rouse them from their lowly bed.

35

For them no more the blazing hearth shall burn,
Or busy housewife ply her evening care:
No children run to lisp their sire's return,
Or climb his knees the envied kiss to share.

Oft did the harvest to their sickle yield,
Their furrow oft the stubborn glebe has broke;
How jocund did they drive their team afield!
How bowed the woods beneath their sturdy stroke!

Let not Ambition mock their useful toil,
Their homely joys and destiny obscure;
Nor Grandeur hear, with a disdainful smile,
The short and simple annals of the poor.

The boast of heraldry, the pomp of power,
And all that beauty, all that wealth e'er gave,
Awaits alike the inevitable hour.
The paths of glory lead but to the grave.

Heraclitus

[WILLIAM CORY]

They told me, Heraclitus, they told me you were dead,
They brought me bitter news to hear and bitter tears to shed.
I wept as I remembered how often you and I
Had tired the sun with talking and sent him down the sky.

And now thou art lying, my dear old Carian guest,
A handful of grey ashes, long, long ago at rest,
Still are thy pleasant voices, thy nightingales, awake;
For Death, he taketh all away, but them he cannot take.

The Walrus and the Carpenter resting
John Tenniel

The Walrus and the Carpenter

[LEWIS CARROLL]

The sun was shining on the sea,
  Shining with all his might:
He did his very best to make
  The billows smooth and bright –
And this was odd, because it was
  The middle of the night.

The moon was shining sulkily,
  Because she thought the sun
Had got no business to be there
  After the day was done –
'It's very rude of him,' she said,
  'To come and spoil the fun!'

The sea was wet as wet could be,
  The sands were dry as dry.
You could not see a cloud, because
  No cloud was in the sky:
No birds were flying overhead –
  There were no birds to fly.

The Walrus and the Carpenter
  Were walking close at hand:
They wept like anything to see
  Such quantities of sand:
'If this were only cleared away,'
  They said, 'it *would* be grand!'

'If seven maids with seven mops
  Swept it for half a year,
Do you suppose,' the Walrus said,
  'That they could get it clear?'
'I doubt it,' said the Carpenter,
  And shed a bitter tear.

'O Oysters, come and walk with us!'
  The Walrus did beseech.
'A pleasant walk, a pleasant talk,
  Along the briny beach:
We cannot do with more than four,
  To give a hand to each.'

The eldest Oyster looked at him,
  But not a word he said:
The eldest Oyster winked his eye,
  And shook his heavy head –
Meaning to say he did not choose
  To leave the oyster-bed.

But four young Oysters hurried up,
  All eager for the treat:
Their coats were brushed, their faces washed
  Their shoes were clean and neat —
And this was odd, because, you know,
  They hadn't any feet.

Four other Oysters followed them,
  And yet another four;
And thick and fast they came at last,
  And more, and more, and more —
All hopping through the frothy waves,
  And scrambling to the shore.

The Walrus and the Carpenter
  Walked on a mile or so,
And then they rested on a rock
  Conveniently low:
And all the little Oysters stood
  And waited in a row.

'The time has come,' the Walrus said,
  'To talk of many things:
Of shoes — and ships — and sealing wax —
  Of cabbages — and kings —
And why the sea is boiling hot —
  And whether pigs have wings.'

'But wait a bit,' the Oysters cried,
  'Before we have our chat;
For some of us are out of breath,
  And all of us are fat!'
'No hurry!' said the Carpenter.
  They thanked him much for that.

'A loaf of bread,' the Walrus said,
  'Is what we chiefly need:
Pepper and vinegar besides
  Are very good indeed –
Now, if you're ready, Oysters dear,
  We can begin to feed.'

'But not on us!' the Oysters cried,
  Turning a little blue.
'After such kindness that would be
  A dismal thing to do!'
'The night is fine,' the Walrus said,
  'Do you admire the view?

'It was so kind of you to come,
  And you are very nice!'
The Carpenter said nothing but
  'Cut us another slice.
I wish you were not quite so deaf –
  I've had to ask you twice!'

'It seems a shame,' the Walrus said,
  'To play them such a trick.
After we've brought them out so far,
  And made them trot so quick!'
The Carpenter said nothing but
  'The butter's spread too thick!'

'I weep for you,' the Walrus said:
  'I deeply sympathize.'
With sobs and tears he sorted out
  Those of the largest size,
Holding his pocket-handkerchief
  Before his streaming eyes.

 'O Oysters,' said the Carpenter,
 'You've had a pleasant run!
Shall we be trotting home again?'
  But answer came there none –
And this was scarcely odd, because
  They'd eaten every one.

'My name is Ozymandias, king of kings'
Alan Powers

Ozymandias

[PERCY BYSSHE SHELLEY]

I met a traveller from an antique land
Who said: Two vast and trunkless legs of stone
Stand in the desert . . . Near them, on the sand,
Half sunk, a shattered visage lies, whose frown,
And wrinkled lip, and sneer of cold command,
Tell that its sculptor well those passions read
Which yet survive, stamped on these lifeless things,
The hand that mocked them, and the heart that fed:
And on the pedestal these words appear:
'My name is Ozymandias, king of kings:
Look on my works, ye Mighty, and despair!'
Nothing beside remains. Round the decay
Of that colossal wreck, boundless and bare
The lone and level sands stretch far away.

We'll Go No More A-Roving

[LORD BYRON]

So, we'll go no more a-roving
  So late into the night,
Though the heart be still as loving,
  And the moon be still as bright.

For the sword outwears its sheath,
  And the soul wears out the breast,
And the heart must pause to breathe,
  And love itself have rest.

Though the night was made for loving,
  And the day returns too soon,
Yet we'll go no more a-roving
  By the light of the moon.

The Lake Isle of Innisfree

[W.B. YEATS]

I will arise and go now, and go to Innisfree,
And a small cabin build there, of clay and wattles made:
Nine bean-rows will I have there, a hive for the honey-bee,
And live alone in the bee-loud glade.

And I shall have some peace there, for peace comes
                                        dropping slow,
Dropping from the veils of the morning to where the
                                        cricket sings;
There midnight's all a glimmer, and noon a purple glow,
And evening full of the linnet's wings.

I will arise and go now, for always night and day
I hear lake water lapping with low sounds by the shore;
While I stand on the roadway, or on the pavements gray,
I hear it in the deep heart's core.

Leisure

[WILLIAM HENRY DAVIES]

What is this life if, full of care,
We have no time to stand and stare.

No time to stand beneath the boughs
And stare as long as sheep or cows.

No time to see, when woods we pass,
Where squirrels hide their nuts in grass.

No time to see, in broad daylight,
Streams full of stars like skies at night.

No time to turn at Beauty's glance,
And watch her feet, how they can dance.

No time to wait till her mouth can
Enrich that smile her eyes began.

A poor life this if, full of care,
We have no time to stand and stare.

Afternoon rest
E. Evans

Cargoes

[JOHN MASEFIELD]

Quinquireme of Nineveh from distant Ophir
Rowing home to haven in sunny Palestine,
With a cargo of ivory,
And apes and peacocks,
Sandalwood, cedarwood, and sweet white wine.

Stately Spanish galleon coming from the Isthmus,
Dipping through the Tropics by the palm-green shores,
With a cargo of diamonds,
Emeralds, amethysts,
Topazes, and cinnamon, and gold moidores.

Dirty British coaster with a salt-caked smoke stack
Butting through the Channel in the mad March days,
With a cargo of Tyne coal,
Road-rail, pig-lead,
Firewood, iron-ware, and cheap tin trays.

To His Coy Mistress

[ANDREW MARVELL]

Had we but world enough, and time,
This coyness, Lady, were no crime.
We would sit down and think which way
To walk and pass our long love's day.
Thou by the Indian Ganges' side
Shouldst rubies find: I by the tide
Of Humber would complain. I would
Love you ten years before the Flood,
And you should, if you please, refuse
Till the conversion of the Jews.
My vegetable love should grow
Vaster than empires, and more slow;
An hundred years should go to praise
Thine eyes and on thy forehead gaze;
Two hundred to adore each breast;
But thirty thousand to the rest;
An age at least to every part,
And the last age should show your heart;
For, Lady, you deserve this state,
Nor would I love at lower rate.
　But at my back I always hear
Time's wingèd chariot hurrying near;
And yonder all before us lie
Deserts of vast eternity.

51

Thy beauty shall no more be found,
Nor, in thy marble vault, shall sound
My echoing song: then worms shall try
That long preserved virginity,
And your quaint honour turn to dust,
And into ashes all my lust:
The grave's a fine and private place,
But none, I think, do there embrace.
  Now therefore, while the youthful hue
Sits on thy skin like morning dew,
And while thy willing soul transpires
At every pore with instant fires,
Now let us sport us while we may,
And now, like amorous birds of prey,
Rather at once our time devour
Than languish in his slow-chapt power.
Let us roll all our strength and all
Our sweetness up into one ball,
And tear our pleasures with rough strife
Through the iron gates of life:
Thus, though we cannot make our sun
Stand still, yet we will make him run.

Courting
On a plate bought in Devon

The Book-Hunter

[FRANK DEMPSTER SHERMAN]

A cup of coffee, eggs, and rolls
Sustain him on his morning strolls:
Unconscious of the passers-by,
He trudges on with downcast eye;
He wears a queer old hat and coat,
Suggestive of a style remote;
His manner is preoccupied –
A shambling gait, from side to side.
For him the sleek, bright-windowed shop
Is all in vain – he does not stop.
His thoughts are fixed on dusty shelves
Where musty volumes hide themselves –
Rare prints of poetry and prose,
And quaintly lettered folios –
Perchance a parchment manuscript,
In some forgotten corner slipped,
Or monk-illumined missal bound
In vellum with brass clasps around;
These are the pictured things that throng
His mind the while he walks along.
A dingy street, a cellar dim,
With book-lined walls, suffices him.
The dust is white upon his sleeves;
He turns the yellow, dog-eared leaves

With just the same religious look
That priests give to the Holy Book.
He does not heed the stifling air
If so he find a treasure there.
He knows rare books, like precious wines,
Are hidden where the sun ne'er shines;
For him delicious flavours dwell
In books as in old Muscatel;
He finds in features of the type
A clew to prove the grape was ripe.
And when he leaves this dismal place,
Behold, a smile lights up his face!
Upon his cheeks a genial glow –
Within his hand Boccaccio,
A first edition worn with age,
'Firenze' on the title-page.

La Belle Dame Sans Merci

[JOHN KEATS]

'O what can ail thee, knight-at-arms,
   Alone and palely loitering?
The sedge has withered from the lake,
   And no birds sing.

'O what can ail thee, knight-at-arms,
   So haggard and so woe-begone?
The squirrel's granary is full,
   And the harvest's done.

'I see a lily on thy brow
   With anguish moist and fever dew;
And on thy cheek a fading rose
   Fast withereth too.'

'I met a lady in the meads,
   Full beautiful – a faery's child,
Her hair was long, her foot was light,
   And her eyes were wild.

'I made a garland for her head,
   And bracelets too, and fragrant zone;
She looked at me as she did love,
   And made sweet moan.

'I set her on my pacing steed
  And nothing else saw all day long,
For sideways would she lean, and sing
  A faery's song.

'She found me roots of relish sweet,
  And honey wild and manna dew,
And sure in language strange she said,
  'I love thee true!'

'She took me to her elfin grot,
  And there she wept and sighed full sore;
And there I shut her wild, wild eyes
  With kisses four.

'And there she lullèd me asleep,
  And there I dreamed – Ah! woe betide!
The lastest dream I ever dreamed
  On the cold hill's side.

'I saw pale kings and princes too,
  Pale warriors, death-pale were they all;
Who cried – "La belle Dame sans Merci
  Hath thee in thrall!"

'I saw their starved lips in the gloam
  With horrid warning gapèd wide,
And I awoke and found me here
  On the cold hill's side.

'And this is why I sojourn here
  Alone and palely loitering,
Though the sedge is withered from the lake,
  And no birds sing.'

Kubla Khan

[SAMUEL TAYLOR COLERIDGE]

In Xanadu did Kubla Khan
   A stately pleasure-dome decree:
Where Alph, the sacred river, ran
Through caverns measureless to man
   Down to a sunless sea.
So twice five miles of fertile ground
   With walls and towers were girdled round:
And there were gardens bright with sinuous rills
Where blossomed many an incense-bearing tree;
And here were forests ancient as the hills,
Enfolding sunny spots of greenery.
But O, that deep romantic chasm which slanted
Down the green hill athwart a cedarn cover!
A savage place! as holy and enchanted
As e'er beneath a waning moon was haunted
By woman wailing for her demon-lover!
And from this chasm, with ceaseless turmoil seething,
As if this earth in fast thick pants were breathing,
A mighty fountain momently was forced;
Amid whose swift half-intermitted burst
Huge fragments vaulted like rebounding hail,
Or chaffy grain beneath the thresher's flail:
And 'mid these dancing rocks at once and ever
It flung up momently the sacred river.
Five miles meandering with a mazy motion

59

Through wood and dale the sacred river ran,
Then reached the caverns measureless to man,
And sank in tumult to a lifeless ocean:
And 'mid this tumult Kubla heard from far
Ancestral voices prophesying war!

The shadow of the dome of pleasure
 Floated midway on the waves;
Where was heard the mingled measure
 From the fountain and the caves.
It was a miracle of rare device,
 A sunny pleasure-dome with caves of ice!

A damsel with a dulcimer
 In a vision once I saw:
It was an Abyssinian maid,
 And on her dulcimer she played,
Singing of Mount Abora.
Could I revive within me,
 Her symphony and song,
To such a deep delight 'twould win me,
That with music loud and long,
I would build that dome in air,
That sunny dome! those caves of ice!
And all who heard should see them there,
And all should cry, Beware! Beware!
His flashing eyes, his floating hair!
Weave a circle round him thrice,
 And close your eyes with holy dread,
 For he on honey-dew hath fed,
And drunk the milk of Paradise.

How Pleasant to Know Mr Lear

[EDWARD LEAR]

'How pleasant to know Mr Lear!'
  Who has written such volumes of stuff!
Some think him ill-tempered and queer,
  But a few think him pleasant enough.

His mind is concrete and fastidious,
  His nose is remarkably big;
His visage is more or less hideous,
  His beard it resembles a wig.

He has ears, and two eyes, and ten fingers,
  Leastways if you reckon two thumbs;
Long ago he was one of the singers,
  But now he is one of the dumbs.

He sits in a beautiful parlour,
  With hundreds of books on the wall
He drinks a great deal of Marsala,
  But never gets tipsy at all.

He has many friends, laymen and clerical,
  Old Foss is the name of his cat:
His body is perfectly spherical,
  He weareth a runcible hat.

61

When he walks in a waterproof white,
  The children run after him so!
Calling out, 'He's come out in his night-
  gown, that crazy old Englishman, oh!'

He weeps by the side of the ocean,
  He weeps on the top of the hill;
He purchases pancakes and lotion,
  And chocolate shrimps from the mill.

He reads but he cannot speak Spanish,
  He cannot abide ginger-beer:
Ere the days of his pilgrimage vanish,
  How pleasant to know Mr Lear!

Mr Lear with Old Foss and friends
Edward Lear

The Listeners

[WALTER DE LA MARE]

'Is there anybody there?' said the Traveller,
    Knocking on the moonlit door;
And his horse in the silence champed the grasses
    Of the forest's ferny floor:
And a bird flew up out of the turret,
    Above the Traveller's head:
And he smote upon the door again a second time;
    'Is there anybody there?' he said.
But no one descended to the Traveller;
    No head from the leaf-fringed sill
Leaned over and looked into his grey eyes,
    Where he stood perplexed and still.
But only a host of phantom listeners
    That dwelt in the lone house then
Stood listening in the quiet of the moonlight
    To that voice from the world of men:
Stood thronging the faint moonbeams on the dark stair,
    That goes down to the empty hall,
Harkening in an air stirred and shaken
    By the lonely Traveller's call.
And he felt in his heart their strangeness,
    Their stillness answering his cry,
While his horse moved, cropping the dark turf,
    'Neath the starred and leafy sky;

For suddenly he smote on the door, even
    Louder, and lifted his head: —
'Tell them I came, and no one answered,
    That I kept my word,' he said.
Never the least stir made the listeners,
    Though every word he spake
Fell echoing through the shadowiness of the still house
    From the one man left awake:
Ay, they heard his foot upon the stirrup,
    And the sound of iron on stone,
And how the silence surged softly backward,
    When the plunging hoofs were gone.

Annabel Lee

[EDGAR ALLAN POE]

It was many and many a year ago,
  In a kingdom by the sea,
That a maiden there lived whom you may know
  By the name of Annabel Lee.
And this maiden she lived with no other thought
  Than to love and be loved by me.

I was a child and she was a child
  In this kingdom by the sea:
But we loved with a love that was more than love –
  I and my Annabel Lee,
With a love that the wingèd seraphs of heaven
  Coveted her and me.

And this was the reason that, long ago,
  In this kingdom by the sea,
A wind blew out of a cloud, chilling
  My beautiful Annabel Lee,
So that her high-born kinsmen came
  And bore her away from me,
To shut her up in a sepulchre
  In this kingdom by the sea.

The angels, not half so happy in heaven,
  Went envying her and me –
Yes! that was the reason (as all men know,
  In this kingdom by the sea)
That the wind came out of the cloud one night,
  Chilling and killing my Annabel Lee.

But our love it was stronger by far than the love
  Of those who were older than we –
  Of many far wiser than we –
And neither the angels in heaven above,
  Nor the demons down under the sea,
Can ever dissever my soul from the soul
  Of the beautiful Annabel Lee.

For the moon never beams without bringing me dreams
  Of the beautiful Annabel Lee;
And the stars never rise, but I feel the bright eyes
  Of the beautiful Annabel Lee;
And so, all the night-tide, I lie down by the side
Of my darling – my darling – my life and my bride,
  In the sepulchre there by the sea,
  In her tomb by the sounding sea.

Gipsy Vans

[RUDYARD KIPLING]

Unless you come of the gipsy stock
  That steal by night and day,
Lock your heart with a double lock
  And throw the key away.
Bury it under the blackest stone
  Beneath your father's hearth,
And keep your eyes on your lawful own
  And your feet to the proper path.
     Then you can stand at your door and mock
      When the gipsy-vans come through . . .
     For it isn't right that the Gorgio stock
      Should live as the Romany do.

Unless you come of the gipsy blood
  That takes and never spares,
Bide content with your given good
  And follow your own affairs.
Plough and harrow and roll your land,
  And sow what ought to be sowed;
But never let loose your heart from your hand,
  Nor flitter it down the road!
     Then you can thrive on your boughten food
      As the gipsy-vans come through . . .
     For it isn't nature the Gorgio blood
      Should love as the Romany do.

Unless you carry the gipsy eyes
  That see but seldom weep,
Keep your head from the naked skies
  Or the stars'll trouble your sleep.
Watch your moon through your window-pane
  And take what weather she brews;
But don't run out in the midnight rain
  Nor home in the morning dews.
     Then you can huddle and shut your eyes
      As the gipsy-vans come through . . .
     For it isn't fitting the Gorgio ryes
      Should walk as the Romany do.

Unless you come of the gipsy race
  That counts all time the same,
Be you careful of Time and Place
  And Judgment and Good Name:
Lose your life for to live your life
  The way that you ought to do;
And when you are finished, your God and your wife
  And the Gipsies 'll laugh at you!
     Then you can rot in your burying-place
      As the gipsy-vans come through . . .
     For it isn't reason the Gorgio race
      Should die as the Romany do.

Jim
Who ran away from his Nurse,
and was eaten by a Lion.
[HILAIRE BELLOC]

There was a Boy whose name was Jim;
His Friends were very good to him.
They gave him Tea, and Cakes, and Jam,
And slices of delicious Ham,
And Chocolate with pink inside,
And little tricycles to ride,
And read him stories through and through,
And even took him to the Zoo —
But there it was the dreadful Fate
Befell him, which I now relate.

You know — at least you *ought* to know,
For I have often told you so —
That Children never are allowed
To leave their Nurses in a Crowd;
Now this was Jim's especial foible,
He ran away when he was able,
And on this inauspicious day
He slipped his hand and ran away!
He hadn't gone a yard when —
                    Bang!

With open Jaws, a Lion sprang,
And hungrily began to eat
The Boy: beginning at his feet.

Now just imagine how it feels
When first your toes and then your heels,
And then by gradual degrees,
Your shins and ankles, calves and knees,
Are slowly eaten, bit by bit.
Now wonder Jim detested it!
No wonder that he shouted 'Hi!'
The Honest Keeper heard his cry,
Though very fat, he almost ran
To help the little gentleman.
'Ponto!' he ordered as he came
(For Ponto was the Lion's name),
'Ponto!' he cried, with angry Frown.
'Let go, Sir! Down, Sir! Put it down!'

The Lion made a sudden stop,
He let the Dainty Morsel drop,
And slunk reluctant to his Cage,
Snarling with Disappointed Rage.
But when he bent him over Jim,
The Honest Keeper's Eyes were dim.
The Lion having reached his Head,
The Miserable Boy was dead!

When Nurse informed his Parents, they
Were more Concerned than I can say: –
His Mother, as She dried her eyes,
Said, 'Well – it gives me no surprise,
He would not do as he was told!'
His Father, who was self-controlled,
Bade all the children round attend
To James' miserable end,
And always keep a-hold of Nurse
For fear of finding something worse.

The end in sight

Sea Fever

[JOHN MASEFIELD]

I must go down to the seas again, to the lonely sea and the sky,
And all I ask is a tall ship and a star to steer her by;
And the wheel's kick and the wind's song and the white sail's
                                        shaking,
And a grey mist on the sea's face, and a grey dawn breaking.

I must go down to the seas again, for the call of the running tide
Is a wild call and a clear call that may not be denied;
And all I ask is a windy day with the white clouds flying,
And the flung spray and the blown spume, and the sea-gulls
                                        crying.

I must go down to the seas again, to the vagrant gypsy life,
To the gull's way and the whale's way where the wind's like a
                                        whetted knife;
And all I ask is a merry yarn from a laughing fellow-rover,
And quiet sleep and a sweet dream when the long trick's over.

The twirl and swirl of the dancing girl
Henri Boutz

Tarantella
[Hilaire Belloc]

Do you remember an Inn,
Miranda?
Do you remember an Inn?
And the tedding and the spreading
Of the straw for a bedding,
And the fleas that tease in the High Pyrenees,
And the wine that tasted of the tar,
And the cheers and the jeers of the young muleteers
(Under the vine of the dark verandah)?
Do you remember an Inn, Miranda?
Do you remember an Inn?
And the cheers and the jeers of the young muleteers
Who hadn't got a penny,
And who weren't paying any,
And the hammer at the doors and the Din?
And the Hip! Hop! Hap!
Of the clap
Of the hands to the twirl and the swirl
Of the girl gone chancing,
Glancing,
Dancing,
Backing and advancing,
Snapping of the clapper to the spin
Out and in —
And the Ting, Tong, Tang of the Guitar!

Do you remember an Inn,
Miranda?
Do you remember an Inn?
Never more;
Miranda,
Never more.
Only the high peaks hoar;
And Aragon a torrent at the door.
No sound
In the walls of the Halls where falls
The tread
Of the feet of the dead to the ground.
No sound:
But the boom
Of the far Waterfall like Doom.

Requiems

[CHRISTINA ROSSETTI]

When I am dead, my dearest,
  Sing no sad songs for me;
Plant thou no roses at my head,
  Nor shady cypress tree:
Be the green grass above me
  With showers and dewdrops wet;
And if thou wilt, remember,
  And if thou wilt, forget.

I shall not see the shadows,
  I shall not feel the rain;
I shall not hear the nightingale
  Sing on, as if in pain;
And dreaming through the twilight
  That doth not rise nor set,
Haply I may remember,
  And haply may forget.

The Golden Vanity
[Folk Song]

A ship I have got in the North Country
And she goes by the name of the Golden Vanity,
O I fear she will be taken by a Spanish Galalie,
  And she sails by the Lowlands low.

To the Captain then up-spake the little Cabin boy,
He said, 'What is my fee if the galley I destroy,
O the Spanish Galalie if no more it shall annoy,
  As you sail by the Lowlands low.'

'Of silver and gold I will give to you a store,
And my pretty little daughter that dwelleth on the shore,
Of treasure and of fee as well I'll give to thee galore,
  As we sail by the Lowlands low.'

Then the boy bared his breast, and straightway leapèd in,
And he held all in his hand an augur sharp and thin,
And he swam until he came to the Spanish Galleon,
  As she lay by the Lowlands low.

He bored with the augur, he bored once and twice,
And some were playing cards, and some were playing dice,
When the water flowed in it dazzlèd their eyes,
  As she sank by the Lowlands low.

So the Cabin-boy did swim all to the larboard side,
Saying, 'Captain! take me in, I am drifting with the tide!'
'I will shoot you! I will kill you!' the cruel Captain cried,
  'You may sink by the Lowlands low.'

Then the Cabin-boy did swim all to the starboard side,
Saying, 'Messmates, take me in, I am drifting with the tide!'
Then they laid him on the deck, and he closed his eyes and died,
  As they sailed by the Lowlands low.

They sewed his body up, all in an old cow's hide,
And they cast the gallant Cabin-boy over the ship's side,
And left him without more ado a-drifting with the tide
  And to sink by the Lowlands low.

From The Ballad of Reading Gaol
[OSCAR WILDE]

He did not wear his scarlet coat,
  For blood and wine are red,
And blood and wine were on his hands
  When they found him with the dead,
The poor dead woman whom he loved,
  And murdered in her bed.

He walked amongst the Trial Men
  In a suit of shabby grey;
A cricket cap was on his head,
  And his step seemed light and gay;
But I never saw a man who looked
  So wistfully at the day.

I never saw a man who looked
  With such a wistful eye
Upon that little tent of blue
  Which prisoners call the sky,
And at every drifting cloud that went
  With sails of silver by.

I walked, with other souls in pain,
  Within another ring,
And was wondering if the man had done
  A great or little thing,
When a voice behind me whispered low,
  'That fellow's got to swing.'

Dear Christ! the very prison walls
  Suddenly seemed to reel,
And the sky above my head became
  Like a casque of scorching steel;
And, though I was a soul in pain,
  My pain I could not feel.

I only knew what hunted thought
  Quickened his step, and why
He looked upon the garish day
  With such a wistful eye;
The man had killed the thing he loved,
  And so he had to die.

Yet each man kills the thing he loves,
  By each let this be heard,
Some do it with a bitter look,
  Some with a flattering word.
The coward does it with a kiss,
  The brave man with a sword!

. . .

He did not wring his hands, as do
  Those witless men who dare
To try to rear the changeling Hope
  In the cave of black Despair:
He only looked upon the sun,
  And drank the morning air.

. . .

And I and all the souls in pain,
  Who tramped the other ring,
Forgot if we ourselves had done
  A great or little thing,
And watched with gaze of dull amaze
  The man who had to swing.

. . .

That night the empty corridors
  Were full of forms of Fear,
And up and down the iron town
  Stole feet we could not hear,
And through the bars that hide the stars
  White faces seemed to peer.

He lay as one who lies and dreams
  In a pleasant meadow-land,
The watchers watched him as he slept,
  And could not understand
How one could sleep so sweet a sleep
  With a hangman close at hand.

But there is no sleep when men must weep
  Who never yet have wept:
So we – the fool, the fraud, the knave –
  That endless vigil kept,
And through each brain on hands of pain
  Another's terror crept.

Alas! it is a fearful thing
  To feel another's guilt!
For, right within, the Sword of Sin
  Pierced to its poisoned hilt,
And as molten lead were the tears we shed
  For the blood we had not spilt.

The warders with their shoes of felt
  Crept by each padlocked door,
And peeped and saw, with eyes of awe,
  Grey figures on the floor,
And wondered why men knelt to pray
  Who never prayed before.

. . .

At six o'clock we cleaned our cells,
  At seven all was still,
But the sough and swing of a mighty wing
  The prison seemed to fill,
For the Lord of Death with icy breath
  Had entered in to kill.

He did not pass in purple pomp,
  Nor ride a moon-white steed.
Three yards of cord and a sliding board
  Are all the gallows need:
So with rope of shame the Herald came
  To do the secret deed.

. . .

We waited for the stroke of eight:
  Each tongue was thick with thirst:
For the stroke of eight is the stroke of Fate
  That makes a man accursed,
And Fate will use a running noose
  For the best man and the worst.

. . .

With sudden shock the prison-clock
  Smote on the shivering air,
And from all the gaol rose up a wail
  Of impotent despair,
Like the sound that frightened marshes hear
  From some leper in his lair.

And as one sees most fearful things
  In the crystal of a dream,
We saw the greasy hempen rope
  Hooked to the blackened beam,
And heard the prayer the hangman's snare
  Strangled into a scream.

And all the woe that moved him so
  That he gave that bitter cry,
And the wild regrets, and the bloody sweats,
  None knew so well as I:
For he who lives more lives than one
  More deaths than one must die.

     . . .

In Reading gaol by Reading town
  There is a pit of shame,
And in it lies a wretched man
  Eaten by teeth of flame,
In a burning winding-sheet he lies,
  And his grave has got no name.

And there, till Christ call forth the dead,
  In silence let him lie:
No need to waste the foolish tear,
  Or heave the windy sigh:
The man had killed the thing he loved,
  And so he had to die.

And all men kill the thing they love,
  By all let this be heard,
Some do it with a bitter look,
  Some with a flattering word,
The coward does it with a kiss,
  The brave man with a sword!

The Old Man's Comforts and
How He Gained Them

[ROBERT SOUTHEY]

'You are old, Father William,' the young man cried,
  'The few locks which are left you are grey;
You are hale, Father William, a hearty old man,
  Now tell me the reason, I pray.'

'In the days of my youth,' Father William replied,
  'I remembered that youth would fly fast,
And abused not my health and my vigour at first,
  That I never might need them at last.'

'You are old, Father William,' the young man cried,
  'And pleasures with youth pass away;
And yet you lament not the days that are gone,
  Now tell me the reason, I pray.'

'In the days of my youth,' Father William replied,
  'I remembered that youth could not last;
I thought of the future, whatever I did,
  That I never might grieve for the past.'

'You are old, Father William,' the young man cried,
  'And life must be hastening away;
You are cheerful, and love to converse upon death,
  Now tell me the reason, I pray.'

'I am cheerful, young man,' Father William replied,
  'Let the cause thy attention engage;
In the days of my youth I remembered my God,
  And He hath not forgotten my age.'

Father William performing
John Tenniel

You are old, Father William

[LEWIS CARROLL]

'You are old, Father William,' the young man said,
'And your hair has become very white;
And yet you incessantly stand on your head –
Do you think, at your age, it is right?'

'In my youth,' Father William replied to his son,
'I feared it might injure the brain;
But, now that I'm perfectly sure I have none,
Why, I do it again and again.'

'You are old,' said the youth, 'as I mentioned before,
And have grown most uncommonly fat;
Yet you turned a back-somersault in at the door –
Pray, what is the reason of that?'

'In my youth,' said the sage, as he shook his grey locks,
'I kept all my limbs very supple
By the use of this ointment – one shilling the box –
Allow me to sell you a couple?'

'You are old,' said the youth, 'and your jaws are too weak
For anything tougher than suet;
Yet you finished the goose, with the bones and the beak –
Pray, how did you manage to do it?'

'In my youth,' said his father, 'I took to the law,
    And argued each case with my wife;
And the muscular strength, which it gave to my jaw,
    Has lasted the rest of my life.'

'You are old,' said the youth, 'one would hardly suppose
    That your eye was as steady as ever;
Yet you balanced an eel on the end of your nose –
    What made you so awfully clever?'

'I have answered three questions, and that is enough,'
    Said his father. 'Don't give yourself airs!
Do you think I can listen all day to such stuff?
    Be off, or I'll kick you downstairs!'

The Statesman

[HILAIRE BELLOC]

I knew a man who used to say,
Not once but twenty times a day,
That in the turmoil and the strife
(His very words) of Public Life
The thing of ultimate effect
Was Character — not Intellect.
He therefore was at strenuous pains
To atrophy his puny brains
And registered success in this
Beyond the dreams of avarice,
Till, when he had at last become
Blind, paralytic, deaf and dumb,
Insensible and cretinous,
He was admitted ONE OF US.
They therefore, (meaning Them by 'They')
His colleagues of the N.C.A.,
The T.U.C., the I.L.P.,
Appointed him triumphantly
To bleed the taxes of a clear
200,000 Francs a year
(Swiss), as the necessary man
For Conferences at Lausanne,
Geneva, Basle, Locarno, Berne:
A salary which he will earn,
Yes — *earn* I say — until he Pops,
Croaks, passes in his checks and Stops:—
When he will be remembered for
A week, a month, or even more.

The Burial of Sir John Moore after Corunna
[CHARLES WOLFE]

Not a drum was heard, not a funeral note,
  As his corpse to the rampart we hurried;
Not a soldier discharged his farewell shot
  O'er the grave where our hero we buried.

We buried him darkly at dead of night,
  The sods with our bayonets turning,
By the struggling moonbeam's misty light
  And the lanthorn dimly burning.

No useless coffin enclosed his breast,
  Not in sheet or in shroud we wound him;
But he lay like a warrior taking his rest
  With his martial cloak around him.

Few and short were the prayers we said,
  And we spoke not a word of sorrow;
But we steadfastly gazed on the face that was dead,
  And we bitterly thought of the morrow.

We thought, as we hollow'd his narrow bed
  And smooth'd down his lonely pillow,
That the foe and the stranger would tread o'er his head,
  And we far away on the billow!

Lightly they'll talk of the spirit that's gone,
  And o'er his cold ashes upbraid him –
But little he'll reck, if they let him sleep on
  In the grave where a Briton has laid him.

But half our heavy task was done
  When the clock struck the hour for retiring;
And we heard the distant and random gun
  That the foe was sullenly firing.

Slowly and sadly we laid him down,
  From the field of his fame fresh and gory;
We carved not a line, and we raised not a stone,
  But we left him alone with his glory.

From Ode to a Nightingale
[JOHN KEATS]

My heart aches, and a drowsy numbness pains
  My sense, as though of hemlock I had drunk,
Or emptied some dull opiate to the drains
  One minute past, and Lethe-wards had sunk:
'Tis not through envy of thy happy lot,
  But being too happy in thy happiness,
    That thou, light-wingèd Dryad of the trees,
      In some melodious plot
  Of beechen green, and shadows numberless,
    Singest of summer in full-throated ease.

O for a draught of vintage! that hath been
  Cooled a long age in the deep-delvèd earth,
Tasting of Flora and the country-green,
  Dance, and Provençal song, and sunburnt mirth!
O for a beaker full of the warm South!
  Full of the true, the blushful Hippocrene,
    With beaded bubbles winking at the brim,
      And purple-stainèd mouth;
  That I might drink, and leave the world unseen,
    And with thee fade away into the forest dim.

Fade far away, dissolve, and quite forget
  What thou among the leaves hast never known,
The weariness, the fever, and the fret
  Here, where men sit and hear each other groan;
Where palsy shakes a few, sad, last grey hairs,
  Where youth grows pale, and spectre-thin, and dies;
    Where but to think is to be full of sorrow
        And leaden-eyed despairs;
  Where Beauty cannot keep her lustrous eyes,
    Or new Love pine at them beyond to-morrow.

Away! away! for I will fly to thee,
  Not charioted by Bacchus and his pards,
But on the viewless wings of Poesy,
  Though the dull brain perplexes and retards:
Already with thee! tender is the night,
  And haply the Queen-Moon is on her throne,
    Clustered around by all her starry Fays;
        But here there is no light,
  Save what from heaven is with the breezes blown
    Through verdurous glooms and winding mossy ways.

Jabberwocky

[LEWIS CARROLL]

'Twas brillig, and the slithy toves
  Did gyre and gimble in the wabe:
All mimsy were the borogoves,
  And the mome raths outgrabe.

'Beware the Jabberwock, my son!
  The jaws that bite, the claws that catch!
Beware the Jubjub bird, and shun
  The frumious Bandersnatch!'

He took his vorpal sword in hand:
  Long time the manxome foe he sought —
So rested he by the Tumtum tree,
  And stood awhile in thought.

And as in uffish thought he stood,
  The Jabberwock, with eyes of flame,
Came whiffling through the tulgey wood,
  And burbled as it came!

One, two! One, two! And through and through
  The vorpal blade went snicker-snack!
He left it dead, and with its head
  He went galumphing back.

95

'And hast thou slain the Jabberwock!
  Come to my arms, my beamish boy!
Oh frabjous day! Callooh! Callay!'
  He chortled in his joy.

'Twas brillig, and the slithy toves
  Did gyre and gimble in the wabe:
All mimsy were the borogoves,
  And the mome raths outgrabe.

The Jabberwock 'came whiffling through
the tulgey wood'
John Tenniel

The Sultan of My Books
[EDMUND GOSSE]

Come hither, my Wither,
  My Suckling, my Dryden!
My Hudibras, hither!
  My Heinsius from Leyden!
Dear Play-books in quarto,
  Fat tomes in brown leather
Stray never too far to
  Come back here together!

I've varied departments
  To give my books shelter;
Shelves, open apartments
  For tomes helter-skelter;
These are artisans' flats, fit
  For common editions, —
I find them, as that's fit,
  Good wholesome positions.

But books that I cherish
  Live under glass cases;
In the waste lest they perish
  I build them oases;
Where gas cannot find them,
  Where worms cannot grapple,
Those panes hold behind them
  My eye and its apple.

98

And here you see flirting
  Fine folks of distinction:
Unique books just skirting
  The verge of extinction;
Old texts with one error
  And long notes upon it;
The 'Magistrates' Mirror'
  (With Nottingham's sonnet);

Tooled Russias to gaze on,
  Moroccos to fondle,
My Denham, in blazon,
  My vellum-backed Vondel,
My Marvell, – a copy
  Was never seen taller, –
My Jones's 'Love Poppy',
  My dear little Waller;

I never upbraid these
  Old periwigged sinners,
Their songs and light ladies,
  Their dances and dinners;
My book-shelf's a haven
  From storms puritanic, –
Why need they be craven?
  Of death they've no panic!

My book-room is little,
  And poor are its treasures;
All pleasures are brittle,
  And so are my pleasures;
But though I shall never
  Be Beckford or Locker,
While Fate does not sever
  The door from the knocker,

No book shall tap vainly
  At latch or at lattice
(If costumed urbanely,
  And worth our care, that is);
In winter or summer,
  My bards in morocco
Shall shield the new comer
  From storm or sirocco.

I might prate thus for pages,
  The theme is so pleasant;
But the gloom of the ages
  Lies on me at present;
All business and fear to
  The cold world I banish.
Hush! like the Ameer, to
  My harem I vanish!

The Wraggle Taggle Gipsies
[ANON]

Three gipsies stood at the Castle gate,
They sang so high, they sang so low,
The lady sate in her chamber late,
Her heart it melted away like snow.

They sang so sweet, they sang so shrill,
That fast her tears began to flow.
And she laid down her silken gown,
Her golden rings and all her show.

She plucked off her high-heeled shoes,
A-made of Spanish leather, O.
She would in the street, with her bare, bare feet;
All out in the wind and weather, O.

O saddle me my milk-white steed,
And go and fetch me my pony, O!
That I may ride and seek my bride,
Who is gone with the wraggle taggle gipsies, O!

O he rode high, and he rode low,
He rode through wood and copses too,
Until he came to an open field,
And there he espied his a-lady, O!

What makes you leave your house and land?
Your golden treasures for to go?
What makes you leave your new-wedded lord,
To follow the wraggle taggle gipsies, O?

What care I for my house and my land?
What care I for my treasure, O?
What care I for my new-wedded lord,
I'm off with the wraggle taggle gipsies, O!

Last night you slept on a goose-feather bed,
With the sheet turned down so bravely, O!
And to-night you'll sleep in a cold open field,
Along with the wraggle taggle gipsies, O!

What care I for a goose-feather bed,
With the sheet turned down so bravely, O!
For to-night I shall sleep in a cold open field,
Along with the wraggle taggle gipsies, O!

O No, John!

[ANON]

On yonder hill there stands a creature;
Who she is I do not know.
I'll go court her for her beauty,
She must answer yes or no.
  O no, John! No, John! No, John! No!

On her bosom are bunches of posies,
On her breast where flowers grow;
If I should chance to touch that posy,
She must answer yes or no.
  O no, John! No, John! No, John! No!

Madam I am come for to court you,
If your favour I can gain;
If you will but entertain me,
Perhaps then I might come again.
  O no, John! No, John! No, John! No!

My husband was a Spanish captain,
Went to sea a month ago;
The very last time we kissed and parted,
Bid me always answer no.
  O no, John! No, John! No, John! No!

Madam in your face is beauty,
In your bosom flowers grow;
In your bedroom there is pleasure,
Shall I view it, yes or no?
  O no, John! No, John! No, John! No!

Madam shall I tie your garter,
Tie it a little above your knee;
If my hand should slip a little farther,
Would you think it amiss of me?
  O no, John! No, John! No, John! No!

My love and I went to bed together,
There we lay till cocks did crow;
Unclose your arms my dearest jewel,
Unclose your arms and let me go.
  O no, John! No, John! No, John! No!

Uphill

[CHRISTINA ROSSETTI]

Does the road wind uphill all the way?
  Yes, to the very end.
Will the day's journey take the whole long day?
  From morn to night, my friend.

But is there for the night a resting-place?
  A roof for when the slow, dark hours begin.
May not the darkness hide it from my face?
  You cannot miss that inn.

Shall I meet other wayfarers at night?
  Those who have gone before.
Then must I knock, or call when just in sight?
  They will not keep you waiting at that door.

Shall I find comfort, travel-sore and weak?
  Of labour you shall find the sum.
Will there be beds for me and all who seek?
  Yea, beds for all who come.

The Way through the Woods

[RUDYARD KIPLING]

They shut the road through the woods
  Seventy years ago.
Weather and rain have undone it again,
  And now you would never know
There was once a path through the woods
  Before they planted the trees,
It is underneath the coppice and the heath,
  And the thin anemones.
  Only the keeper sees
That, where the ring-dove broods,
  And the badgers roll at ease,
There was once a road through the woods.

Yet, if you enter the woods
  Of a summer evening late,
When the night-air cools on the trout-ring'd pools
  Where the otter whistles his mate,
(They fear not men in the woods
  Because they see so few)
You will hear the beat of a horse's feet
  And the swish of a skirt in the dew,
  Steadily cantering through
The misty solitudes,
  As though they perfectly knew
The old lost road through the woods . . .
But there is no road through the woods.

'There was once a road through the woods'
Reynolds Stone

From Horatius

[LORD MACAULAY]

Lars Porsena of Clusium
  By the Nine Gods he swore
That the great house of Tarquin
  Should suffer wrong no more.
By the Nine Gods he swore it,
  And named a trysting day,
And bade his messengers ride forth,
East and west and south and north,
  To summon his array.

East and west and south and north
  The messengers ride fast,
And tower and town and cottage
  Have heard the trumpet's blast.
Shame on the false Etruscan
  Who lingers in his home,
When Porsena of Clusium
  Is on the march for Rome.

The horsemen and the footmen
  Are pouring in amain
From many a stately market-place;
  From many a fruitful plain;
From many a lonely hamlet,
  Which, hid by beech and pine,
Like an eagle's nest, hangs on the crest
  Of purple Apennine.

. . .

I wis, in all the Senate,
  There was no heart so bold,
But sore it ached, and fast it beat,
  When that ill news was told.
Forthwith up rose the Consul,
  Up rose the Fathers all;
In haste they girded up their gowns,
  And hied them to the wall.

They held a council standing
  Before the River-Gate;
Short time was there, ye may well guess,
  For musing or debate.
Out spake the Consul roundly:
  'The bridge must straight go down;
For, since Janiculum is lost,
  Nought else can save the town.'

Just then a scout came flying,
  All wild with haste and fear:
'To arms! to arms! Sir Consul;
  Lars Porsena is here.'
On the low hills to westward
  The Consul fixed his eye,
And saw the swarthy storm of dust
  Rise fast along the sky.

. . .

But the Consul's brow was sad,
  And the Consul's speech was low,
And darkly looked he at the wall,
  And darkly at the foe.
'Their van will be upon us
  Before the bridge goes down;
And if they once may win the bridge,
  What hope to save the town?'

Then out spake brave Horatius,
  The Captain of the gate:
'To every man upon this earth
  Death cometh soon or late.
And how can man die better
  Than facing fearful odds,
For the ashes of his father
  And the temples of his Gods.

. . .

'Hew down the bridge, Sir Consul,
  With all the speed ye may;
I, with two more to help me,
  Will hold the foe in play.
In yon strait path a thousand
  May well be stopped by three.
Now who will stand on either hand,
  And keep the bridge with me?'

Then out spake Spurius Lartius;
  A Ramnian proud was he:
'Lo, I will stand at thy right hand,
  And keep the bridge with thee.'
And out spake strong Herminius;
  Of Titian blood was he:
'I will abide on thy left side,
  And keep the bridge with thee.'

'Horatius,' quoth the Consul,
  'As thou sayest, so let it be.'
And straight against the great array
  Forth went the dauntless Three.
For Romans in Rome's quarrel
  Spared neither land nor gold,
Nor son nor wife, nor limb nor life,
  In the brave days of old.

. . .

Now while the Three were tightening
  Their harness on their backs,
The Consul was the foremost man
  To take in hand an axe:
And Fathers mixed with Commons
  Seized hatchet, bar, and crow,
And smote upon the planks above,
  And loosed the props below.

The holding of the bridge
George Scharf Jun.

Meanwhile the Tuscan army
  Right glorious to behold,
Came flashing back the noonday light,
Rank behind rank, like surges bright
  Of a broad sea of gold.
Four hundred trumpets sounded
  A peal of warlike glee,
As that great host, with measured tread,
And spears advanced, and ensigns spread,
Rolled slowly towards the bridge's head,
  Where stood the dauntless Three.

The Three stood calm and silent
  And looked upon the foes,
And a great shout of laughter
  From all the vanguard rose:
And forth three chiefs came spurring
  Before that deep array;
To earth they sprang, their swords they drew,
And lifted high their shields, and flew
  To win the narrow way;

Aunus from green Tifernum,
  Lord of the Hill of Vines;
And Seius, whose eight hundred slaves
  Sicken in Ilva's mines;
And Picus, long to Clusium
  Vassal in peace and war,
Who led to fight his Umbrian powers
From that grey crag where, girt with towers,
The fortress of Nequinum lowers
  O'er the pale waves of Nar.

Stout Lartius hurled down Aunus
　Into the stream beneath:
Herminius struck at Seius,
　And clove him to the teeth:
At Picus brave Horatius
　Darted one fiery thrust;
And the proud Umbrian's gilded arms
　Clashed in the bloody dust.

Then Ocnus of Falerii
　Rushed on the Roman Three;
And Lausulus of Urgo,
　The rover of the sea;
And Aruns of Volsinium,
　Who slew the great wild boar,
The great wild boar that had his den
Amidst the reeds of Cosa's fen,
And wasted fields, and slaughtered men,
　Along Albinia's shore.

Herminius smote down Aruns:
　Lartius laid Ocnus low:
Right to the heart of Lausulus
　Horatius sent a blow.
'Lie there,' he cried, 'fell pirate!
　No more, aghast and pale,
From Ostia's walls the crowd shall mark
The track of thy destroying bark.
No more Campania's hinds shall fly
To woods and caverns when they spy
　Thy thrice accursed sail.'

But now no sound of laughter
  Was heard amongst the foes.
A wild and wrathful clamour
  From all the vanguard rose.
Six spears' lengths from the entrance
  Halted the deep array,
And for a space no man came forth
  To win the narrow way.

But hark! the cry is Astur:
  And lo! the ranks divide;
And the great Lord of Luna
  Comes with his stately stride.
Upon his ample shoulders
  Clangs loud the four-fold shield,
And in his hand he shakes the brand
  Which none but he can wield.

He smiled on those bold Romans
  A smile serene and high;
He eyed the flinching Tuscans,
  And scorn was in his eye.
Quoth he, 'The she-wolf's litter
  Stand savagely at bay:
But will ye dare to follow,
  If Astur clears the way?'

Then, whirling up his broadsword
    With both hands to the height,
He rushed against Horatius,
    And smote with all his might.
With shield and blade Horatius
    Right deftly turned the blow.
The blow, though turned, came yet too nigh;
It missed his helm, but gashed his thigh:
The Tuscans raised a joyful cry
    To see the red blood flow.

He reeled, and on Herminius
    He leaned one breathing-space;
Then, like a wild cat mad with wounds,
    Sprang right at Astur's face.
Through teeth, and skull, and helmet,
    So fierce a thrust he sped,
The good sword stood a hand-breadth out
    Behind the Tuscan's head.

And the great Lord of Luna
    Fell at that deadly stroke,
As falls on Mount Alvernus
    A thunder-smitten oak.
Far o'er the crashing forest
    The giant arms lie spread;
And the pale augurs, muttering low,
    Gaze on the blasted head.

On Astur's throat Horatius
  Right firmly pressed his heel,
And thrice and four times tugged amain,
  Ere he wrenched out the steel.
'And see,' he cried, 'the welcome,
  Fair guests, that waits you here!
What noble Lucumo comes next
  To taste our Roman cheer?'

But at his haughty challenge
  A sullen murmur ran,
Mingled of wrath, and shame, and dread,
  Along that glittering van.
There lacked not men of prowess,
  Nor men of lordly race;
For all Etruria's noblest
  Were round the fatal place.

But all Etruria's noblest
  Felt their hearts sink to see
On the earth the bloody corpses,
  In the path the dauntless Three:
And, from the ghastly entrance
  Where those bold Romans stood,
All shrank, like boys who unaware,
Ranging the woods to start a hare,
Come to the mouth of the dark lair
Where, growling low, a fierce old bear
  Lies amidst bones and blood.

Was none who would be foremost
   To lead such dire attack;
But those behind cried 'Forward!'
   But those before cried 'Back!'
And backward now and forward
   Wavers the deep array;
And on the tossing sea of steel,
To and fro the standards reel;
And the victorious trumpet-peal
   Dies fitfully away.

. . .

But meanwhile axe and lever
   Have manfully been plied;
And now the bridge hangs tottering
   Above the boiling tide.
'Come back, come back, Horatius!'
   Loud cried the Fathers all.
'Back, Lartius! back, Herminius!
   Back, ere the ruin fall!'

Back darted Spurius Lartius;
   Herminius darted back:
And, as they passed, beneath their feet
   They felt the timbers crack.
But when they turned their faces,
   And on the farther shore
Saw brave Horatius stand alone,
   They would have crossed once more.

But with a crash like thunder
  Fell every loosened beam,
And, like a dam, the mighty wreck
  Lay right athwart the stream:
And a long shout of triumph
  Rose from the walls of Rome,
As to the highest turret-tops
  Was splashed the yellow foam.

And, like a horse unbroken
  When first he feels the rein,
The furious river struggled hard,
  And tossed his tawny mane;
And burst the curb, and bounded,
  Rejoicing to be free;
And whirling down, in fierce career,
Battlement, and plank, and pier,
  Rushed headlong to the sea.

Alone stood brave Horatius,
  But constant still in mind;
Thrice thirty thousand foes before,
  And the broad flood behind.
'Down with him!' cried false Sextus,
  With a smile on his pale face.
'Now yield thee,' cried Lars Porsena,
  'Now yield thee to our grace.'

Round turned he, as not deigning
  Those craven ranks to see;
Nought spake he to Lars Porsena,
  To Sextus nought spake he;
But he saw on Palatinus
  The white porch of his home;
And he spake to the noble river
  That rolls by the towers of Rome.

'Oh, Tiber! father Tiber!
  To whom the Romans pray,
A Roman's life, a Roman's arms,
  Take thou in charge this day!'
So he spake, and speaking sheathed
  The good sword by his side,
And with his harness on his back,
  Plunged headlong in the tide.

No sound of joy or sorrow
  Was heard from either bank;
But friends and foes in dumb surprise,
With parted lips and straining eyes,
  Stood gazing where he sank;
And when above the surges
  They saw his crest appear,
All Rome sent forth a rapturous cry,
And even the ranks of Tuscany
  Could scarce forbear to cheer.

Horatius plunges in
George Scharf Jun.

But fiercely ran the current,
  Swollen high by months of rain:
And fast his blood was flowing;
  And he was sore in pain,
And heavy with his armour,
  And spent with changing blows:
And oft they thought him sinking,
  But still again he rose.

Never, I ween, did swimmer,
  In such an evil case,
Struggle through such a raging flood
  Safe to the landing place:
But his limbs were borne up bravely
  By the brave heart within,
And our good father Tiber
  Bare bravely up his chin.

. . .

And now he feels the bottom;
  Now on dry earth he stands;
Now round him throng the Fathers
  To press his gory hands;
And now with shouts and clapping,
  And noise of weeping loud,
He enters through the River-Gate,
  Borne by the joyous crowd.

They gave him of the corn-land,
  That was of public right,
As much as two strong oxen
  Could plough from morn till night;
And they made a molten image,
  And set it up on high,
And there it stands unto this day
  To witness if I lie.

It stands in the Comitium,
  Plain for all folk to see;
Horatius in his harness,
  Halting upon one knee:
And underneath is written,
  In letters all of gold,
How valiantly he kept the bridge
  In the brave days of old.

Love's Secret
[WILLIAM BLAKE]

Never seek to tell thy love,
  Love that never told can be;
For the gentle wind doth move
  Silently, invisibly.

I told my love, I told my love,
  I told her all my heart,
Trembling, cold, in ghastly fears.
  Ah! she did depart!

Soon after she was gone from me,
  A traveller came by,
Silently, invisibly:
  He took her with a sigh.

PERSONAL FAVOURITES

The next two pages
are for listing your
own favourites

ACKNOWLEDGEMENTS

Little did I realize that *A Gentleman Publisher's Commonplace Book* would whet my appetite for more. To compile, edit and design a book while carrying on my normal publishing activities was not easy for those around me. I must therefore start with a special thanks to my colleagues for being so long-suffering during the creation of this volume. I would also like to thank Alan Powers and Peter Campbell for responding so imaginatively to my request for illustrations for 'Ozymandias' and 'Birds, Bags, Bears and Buns', and Val Biro, Janet Stone (on behalf of Reynolds Stone) and others for permission to use their wood engravings and illustrations.

But above all my thanks must go to Jeff Fisher (both friend and outstanding designer) who, the moment I described this project, entered fully into the spirit of it with creative enthusiasm. The jacket (combining humour with fine style), the title page and the endpapers are the making of the book. The artwork will find a deserving place alongside that of Eric Ravilious, Edward Bawden, John Piper and others in the Murray archive for future generations to admire.

Finally a thank-you to the owners of the copyright of those poems as yet not in the public domain (or which entered it briefly before the EU restored their copyright for a few more years): A.P.Watt on behalf of the National Trust for 'The Way through the Woods' and 'Gipsy Vans' by Rudyard Kipling and on behalf of Michael Yeats for 'The Lake Isle of Innisfree' by W.B.Yeats; Peters, Fraser and Dunlop on behalf of the Estate of Hilaire Belloc for 'The Frog', 'Jim', 'Tarantella' and 'The Statesman'; and the Society of Authors on behalf of the Estate of A.E.Housman for 'When I was One-and-Twenty', the Estate of Walter de la Mare for 'The Listeners', and the Estate of John Masefield for 'Cargoes' and 'Sea Fever'.